THE H.H. HOLMES CONFESSIONS

THE H.H. HOLMES CONFESSIONS

FELIX NORTHWOOD

CONTENTS

CHAPTER 1

Introduction to H.H. Holmes

America's first serial killer, Herman Mudgett, better known as H.H. Holmes, comes to the story through a combination of self-narrative, official transcripts of the lengthy courtroom proceedings, and personal interviews from the Chicago Tribune. Holmes is infamous for his role as a hotelier turned murderer, with a despicably convenient hotel during the Chicago World's Fair of 1893, but for the most part, the reader gets much more of his side of the story as well as coverage of the courtroom proceedings consisting of his witnesses and the more horrifying testimony of the survivors of his hotel and other buildings in Chicago which he had murdered unfortunate souls within. It is impossible to linger too long in the rooms of H. H. Holmes. His daily costume change is drained out of the scene, leaving only himself, his private acts, and *gasp* himself with himself alone. This convergence at the fold keeps his entire confession aloft, laboriously animate.

Before Ted Bundy, there was Dr. H. H. Holmes. This is the confession of H. H. Holmes, America's first serial killer. Terrible as it is in its organization and manner, it is nonetheless such an extraordinary production that it immediately carries his narrative to the realm of the exceptional; again and again we meet accounts of the crimes of seemingly no worse a sort than kindness, carried off by virtue of the splendor of its referent.

Early Life and Background

Herman Webster Mudgett, better known by the alias H.H. Holmes, was an American con artist, bigamist, and serial killer whose namesake has become a byword for evil. Little is known of his background before he arrived in Chicago in the early 1880s. He was born in Gilmanton, New Hampshire, and he married Clara Lovering of Alton, New Hampshire, on July 4th, 1878, even though he had not divorced his first wife, the former Clara A. Gibbs of Scarborough, Maine. Holmes had a son with his first wife, who graduated from the University of Michigan Medical School in 1884. Holmes spent most of his earnings as a doctor, which are uncertain, especially because his own story suggested he started in medicine by stealing and selling cadavers.

Herman Mudgett was admitted to the University of Vermont, College of Medicine at Burlington in July 1882. He practiced in New Hampshire and Maine for two years before coming to Chicago. While at university, he pursued a course in Pharmacy, and he supported Clara and her son by working as a drug clerk in the summers, as a subscription agent, and doing odd jobs in college. During those college years, he developed an unusual friendship with Tom Toomey. Mudgett had a college girlfriend by the name of Mary Howard, who he apparently made love to on one occasion. She became pregnant, but it is uncertain whether she miscarried or gave birth, what the sex of the baby was, or what happened to it. Mudgett was not charged with any responsibility for this. Mary died some time later.

CHAPTER 2

The Murder Castle

The H.H. Holmes Confessions: Inside the Mind of America's First Maximum Serial Killer, which will provide readers for the first time ever with the transcripts of Holmes' written and spoken confession, enabling future generations of researchers, readers, and historians alike the unparalleled opportunity to allow his words to speak for themselves in crafting their own solution to the case, is now available for pre-order.

The now-infamous "Murder Castle," the three-story architectural monstrosity H.H. Holmes designed and had built in Chicago's Englewood neighborhood, was constructed in a specifically designed manner that it was created to serve the sinister purpose it was ultimately altered, built, and used for by Holmes: primarily as a macabre labyrinth designed to allay the fears of its unwitting "guests" and keep them absolutely convinced that their help in disappearing for the promise of a seemingly innocent experiment would prove beneficial. Holmes' construction included airtight apartments and offices and used chutes that relied on principles of negative air pressure to ensure that any foul air and gases would be unable to penetrate the chambers and noticeable to no one. The chutes not only acted as ventricles for the primary gas-laden building but would provide Holmes a convenient and efficacious method to remove the resulting human remains with salvific convenience. In the words of Dr. Patrick Quinlan, an expert on the architectural structure of the building, "There are signs that some of the stains were transported here in solution."

In essence, the Castle was equipped with the very first criminal laboratory, complete with the facilities and appliances that were needed to do the wholesale job of maiming, mangling, and obliterating the bodies of his victims. To chroniclers, authors of the time and since, the very labyrinthine nature of the structure holds a deep fascination and curiosity in that the tangled warren was not built as much for the maximum convenience of the victims as it was for the total satisfaction of the demon's vanity. And it was this very vanity that would certainly contribute to and ultimately play the part in his insistence of having the building constructed with a "blind" third floor and many other peculiar accommodations.

Construction and Layout

The castle Holmes created, which came to be called The Castle, was – for its time – an architectural wonder that housed some of the most horrifying secrets. The three-story building was designed in a terraced manner and covered an entire block, or, to be exact, the 1600 block of Chicago's South Wallace Avenue. The Castle was Dragon Style and reportedly looked like a hotel. In addition to being visually stunning, it was architecturally unusual. The immense first floor was built with glistening white enameled brick, while the second-floor facade was amber. Three-story towers onto which guests could intake all the year old filth of South State Street thrust through the ground floor.

This unusual layout inside the magnificent outer castle designed by Holmes himself. On the first floor, there were a number of leased storefronts, among them a drug store that occupied the northwest corner of the building. On the second floor lay a vast rabbit warren of tiny one and two-room apartments and bland office areas. Most of these rooms were vault-locked and none had windows. In the massive basement, which alone covered the lot, was the grisly stuff of nightmares. The well or whatever it was and the small brightly-lit laboratory were only one side of the haven Holmes created down here. The other side was a crypt or a vault, roughly 17,000 feet of dark, twisted, airless crypt with a sump in the gory center shaped in a wedding cake design – he called it. Holmes had even incorporated greased drain-line rivulets and purpose-built ovens. The Castle was a recurved labyrinth fashioned to obscure what lay behind its contents, or what did not.

CHAPTER 3

Modus Operandi

There have been few homicides in history - the Ripper case in Whitechapel is the only one that comes to mind - which have attracted such widespread interest from the residents of a city as did the homicide of Mary Holland in Philadelphia, and signs of the most acute degree of public anxiety were apparent not only over all of Pennsylvania but in many other States. The infamous H. H. Holmes, murderer of six in Chicago, confessed to seventy-six killings from New Hampshire to Florida between the years of 1887 and 1894. However, only twenty-seven of these confessions have been verified as a possibility of fact. Who better to throw light upon Holmes' methods and motives, his reason for killing this most kindly old lady, than Holmes himself?

Infamy is notoriety, this is true; however, notable only to those who recognize their villainy as outstanding. Criminals are a solitary lot, and all believe in retroverted opinion. Nemo me impune lacessit. In publishing such as he committed and confessing four murders not charged against him, Holmes further solidified his place in the gallery of infamous and sowed enough seeds of doubt to ensure a phantom of malfeasance ruined with the unfathomable aura of eternal enigma in pulp and print. The perfidious paths of the psychopathic multicides is not calculated and clear immediately to the reader. In the example which follows, veiled amongst denials, misnomers, red herrings, and indirect proverbs, the manuscript of Dr. H. Holmes rectifying his fate ended six lives in six weeks in 1893 readily reveals the modus operandi of a psychopathic sacrificer.

Methods of Killing

H. H. Holmes was a man of many schemes. The devilish busybody multitasked as a swindler of grand scale, an insurance fraud artist, and a would-be scion of preeminence through various enterprises. Central to many of his illicit deals, however, was capitalizing on the forces of life and death. Confidentially, Holmes told H. Maynie a comprehensive account of how these skills also rendered him the prolific serial killer of the World's Columbian Exposition - the world would come to know him as America's first serial murderer. Authentication of the diminished claim of 27 victims known but has ever been established. During his interrogations at the Moyamensing Prison in Philadelphia in 1895, the attention of the rest of the world was very slowly beginning to catch up to Philadelphia authorities' recent understanding of the savagery for which he had quietly been under arrest all along.

Holmes' small lips press their words close together. H. Maynie states she can feel their breath on her head. "How many?" "How many—" H. Maynie's is also indistinguishable from Holmes'. Even after reviewing this exchange repeatedly upon it being reported or repeated to her, she remarks with a sour exhalation, "There's too many secrets to even know what he was talking about, when I think about it more and more. And for all the killing, all of the death, I wish I could say there's more of something else, but the only thing I wish was that I had realized, so many people who wouldn't have had to die. I would have run away, I should have never gone into that office!" Holmes' first elaboration offered in his confession was a detailed account of the "various ways" he secured the "extinguishments of the lives he failed."

CHAPTER 4

The Investigation and Arrest

The investigation of H.H. Holmes was as unique as the killer himself. It was a flurry of questions and searches, leads and frustration, spread out across hundreds of miles in numerous states. Law-enforcement officials, amateur sleuths, hired detectives, and family members attempted to track the multiple lives of the fiend down, in order to unknowingly rescue one or more women who were either still alive or had been in Holmes' clutches before meeting a bloody demise. Holmes' sense of humor never faltered during this phase of the inquiries. It was revealed that he had several alibis for various days of the World's Fair, which prosecutors had already anticipated, and he shamelessly played the role of the afraid witness whose physiognomy couldn't possibly resemble his own.

The Lodge kept a grand jury busy for most of 1895, as arguments were heard regarding the validity of the murder indictments presented by the prosecutor. Political infighting between the party of reformers and the party of industrialists forced the case from court to court until a ruling was at last scheduled for November 4, 1895. It was on the eve of this date that Holmes, held on the single charge of murdering Howard Pitezel in spite of his previous confessions, was moved from Moyamensing Jail just outside of Philadelphia to Moyamensing Prison in the same building. There was an attempt on the part of his lawyers to introduce a writ of habeas corpus in order to preempt any other maneuver that the court might have used to remove the case from the dockets yet again, but it was no good on account of the lateness of the hour.

Capture and Initial Suspicions

The Crime of the Century, the Murder Castle, the Wicked Doctor. H.H. Holmes is one of the most notorious serial killers in American history. In "The H.H. Holmes Confessions," Holmes narrates his life, largely detailing the development and construction of his three-story hotel in Chicago, dubbed the "Murder Castle" by Mikita Brottman, who edited the text and provided an extensive introduction and notes. The text concludes with the murder of Howard Pitezel and the impending investigation into the insurance money Holmes received. Holmes was captured and taken into police custody in late 1894. The detectives who caught him believed him to possibly be Jack the Ripper; at the time of his arrest, Holmes was suspected of only a few murders, most notably his caretaker, Benjamin Pitezel, and three of Pitezel's children. His crimes were discovered only when he attempted to collect on a life insurance policy he purchased for the children. When the insurance agents got suspicious, Holmes took the three Pitezel children and went on the run. It wasn't until after he was captured and confessing that 30 murders were unearthed in Chicago and Indianapolis.

In summer 1894, Holmes expressed a desire to pursue graduate study in Europe, setting up a college in Northwest Chicago, the Holmes University, where new students would unknowingly become the patrons of his hotel. In the same issue of the newspaper that reported his capture, another story reported how Holmes had swindled other investors in a previous fraudulent business venture. The Pitezel children and wife were only allowed to stay with Holmes at the hotel in early 1893, two years prior to his capture. Benjamin suspected his wife of having an affair with Holmes, but brushed his suspicions off thinking Holmes was just as repulsive to women as he was, so it could not be true. Benjamin finally left his wife and took the children into police custody when he discovered she was involved with Holmes.

CHAPTER 5

The Confessions

Even early on, newspapers marveled at the phrase "H.H. Holmes Confesses." They wrote that he had told the police everything, without the least hesitation, and that the enormity of Holmes' crimes still beggars belief. After denying he was the fiend for days, and repeatedly altering his story, Holmes' final confession was a sensation in 1896, and it continued to zest true crime readers for decades. Principles in Philadelphia, where he was tried, called Holmes a murderer of the basest—most unmentionable vileness. His then-lawyer called this brief, self-serving work in the American in disparagement of his valuable client.

Holmes never confessed in so many words, for the record; police had been tricked before. But in detail, this new collection delivers his still-astounding ones. After more than a century, here is the complete and authoritative text for both volumes of the so-called Civil War confession, along with Holmes' handwritten confession he gave Philadelphia police and 21 written confessions from various tiny Midwestern jails over 123 days. The Midwestern confessions are, in some ways, the most striking evidence we have of Holmes' true story. Forty victims mentioned in these confessions have never been chronicled. DDMS Benjamin Pitezel is explicit about his sheer bloodlust and desire to murder strangers. Shortly after his Philadelphia confession hit papers, Holmes marveled from his cell at the stir it created in the city. The guy who got my first confession should have been well recompensed, wrote Holmes in a letter that April—truer words were never effused.

Interrogations and Statements

Confession takes many forms for H. H. Holmes, a man accustomed to lying and manipulating every aspect of his life. In the days, months, and years preceding his trial and execution, the investigation and Holmes's subsequent arrest after the disappearance of his business partner, Benjamin Pitezel, thrust Holmes's world into the spotlight, where he was the center of attention. As a result, he gave a variety of statements to the press and city officials, inquiring about the whereabouts of the missing Pitezel children and what had befallen their father. This discussion represents an examination of Holmes in his own element—from the height of his grandiosity in control of the "telling of it all" in his interviews for while awaiting extradition in Boston, to the meeker, more repentant Holmes, crafted for Rev. Ewing's personal eyes shortly before his execution. How Holmes adjusted his tone, and him unspooling the web of lies that got him to this point, is on grand display as we pan forward from 1894 through the beginning of 1896.

The common theme that underlines each of these subsequent interactions seems to be Holmes's protests of his innocence, coupled with steadily increasing paranoia and claims of lunacy on his part. Bringing these statements and some analysis to light now may offer further insight into the mind of H. H. Holmes, and his web of lies, built on a faulty foundation of grandiosity and the belief that one so intelligent could not possibly be caught, if he simply refrained from making a clean statement to officers until he had engineered a way to escape prosecution altogether.

CHAPTER 6

Psychological Analysis

In the analysis of his personality, it appears that Holmes was extroverted and emotionally stable, albeit only in appearance. According to the authors of this book, the notorious serial killer was narcissistic with occasional antisocial leanings. He was sadistic, homicidal, and affected by mania, and he had a predisposition to aggression. There also exists a well-chosen scientific analysis which posits an understanding of all those underlying psychological factors of H.H. Holmes, including the dynamics of his relationship with his unconscious and his own family. A psychoanalytic perspective and evaluation would ascertain the instinctual drives and motivations, and they would show the aims of H.H. Holmes.

Holmes' motivations were predominantly centered upon sex and aggression. He also showed obsessive-compulsive traits. The psychological analyses considered each hypothesis and supported it with coherent instances from various sources, together with case studies, court reports, and news articles, in order to understand the man and the serial killer that H.H. Holmes was. H.H. Holmes is both a criminal and an urban legend. However, in order to comprehend his crimes, one should not limit one's investigation to police reports. Instead, the motives, the life, and the mind of H.H. Holmes should be studied from the perspective of developmental psychology. H.H.

Holmes was a famous con artist who murdered many people. He was noted for his astonishing ability to present himself in public and his fascination with death. When he was finally imprisoned, he counseled police about his psychological problems and began writing his autobiography.

Personality Traits and Motivations

H.H. Holmes perpetrated a murderous spree with a motivational pattern different from some multiple murderers. Rather than killing to cover up his compulsive greed, Holmes appeared to murder for the sheer sense of power, profit, and self-declared godhood derived from his crimes. A significant question remains poorly understood: precisely what personality traits and other motivational factors contributed to Holmes' heinous behavior? Using the "not many, but much" motivational typology, this paper investigates the extent to which the personality traits and motivational types of spree killers and serial murderers offered contributions to Holmes' criminal enterprises. These results are contrasted to research findings of similar multiple murderers, including those findings specific to Holmes. In addition to his grand mal of self-declared divinity, an inability to form the ordinary and reciprocally attractive relationships of other humans may have been overridingly severe and pronounced in his life and impelled considerable proportions of his crimes.

Defining precisely how many multiple murders that Holmes netted is nearly impossible, in large part due to his vast travels in Canada. As is now known to many researchers, there are many such men at any one point in time spread over any number of nations across the globe. It is hoped that studying figures such as H.H. Holmes sheds some light on these rare multi- or single-predators of men. Holmes' adult life was dominated by two preoccupations: engaging in a continuous stream of serial, often repeating and contiguous larcenies without number or precedent. The genuine fine conduct helped maintain, both through the larcenies and through an increasing number of real estate transactions, a lasting mask of respectability. In the summer of 1886, and after Holmes had completed a university term in post-graduate medicine, he realized that he could more readily sate his enormous "political" ambition by the engine of a wholesale and multiform serial murder hobby. Additionally, he could make a net profit from the activity impossible to realize by any of his preceding swindles of insurance companies or of individuals.

CHAPTER 7

Legacy of H.H. Holmes

H.H. Holmes is often noted as "America's first serial killer." As such, he looms large in the public imagination, in the history of criminal profiling, and in the annals of crime. Even now, 125 years after his arrest and confession, relatively little is known about Holmes's actions, motivations, thought processes, or criminological implications of his case, as Holmes provides a "how to" of memoricide. It is for these reasons that it is crucial to discover how an offender is remembered and how his memory continues to impact the world from which he was erased. Such an inquiry can reveal much about the ripple effects of his crimes, of victimization and loss, and of the criminal justice complex in a macroscopic sense.

Holmes has attracted great attention not only because of the heinous crimes he committed but also because of what they were thought to portend. Before he made any confessions, his case was taken up as a key cold-case puzzle, full of exciting medical and forensic details. A human searchlight of inquiry was turned on, an anticipated excitement about being able to directly discover the mind of a madman, and immigrants, secrets, and "innate criminal tendencies" abounding in the mid-1890s. The confirmation of some but not all of a list filled with lurid expectations of criminal intrigue further solidified the case's presence in the area of criminal psychology, forcing an interpretation despite the dearth of evidence from the inner sanctum of the investigator's world in the thief taker or detective's model of crime detection. That he ultimately made a series of confessions, then, is important not as the identification of an offender but because of what it meant concerning the trajectory of criminal profiling and what his name posthumous meant concerning the future of law enforcement.

Impact on Criminal Profiling

The case of H.H. Holmes continues to influence criminal profiling. Though Holmes does not fit the profile of the serial killer constructed in the last few decades, his case has contributed important elements to the art of profiling criminals that are still pertinent today. If modern law enforcement professionals are aware of the history of criminal profiling, they have reason to believe that an untold number of unsolved crimes have been committed by serial predators who own property with hidden trapdoors, poison others systematically, and hold their targets' lives in their hands. Dr. Thomas Harris drew from his awareness of Holmes when he composed the rough outline for the antagonists in his books, Manhunter and Red Dragon.

John Douglas, credited with being one of the godfathers of criminal profiling and acknowledged author of Mindhunter, answers the question of what exactly resides in someone's head when they commit such acts. How did agents begin to probe the minds of individuals who thought and acted in ways polar-opposite to their own? If Holmes helped contribute significant investigation strategies to modern criminal investigation, then the "brutality" and "murder-rate" of the "modern world" would logically aid in controlling "Jacks" the world over. Consider how Jack observed vulnerable women to exploit and murder. Categorizing women would be just as impractical for Jack as for Holmes. With rare exception, no woman thinks, feels, acts, or looks like another, and "Jack" would not find this approach very expedient. Instead, he would deduce a woman's tactics and discoveries by directly observing her individual behavior and contemplating her in vivo.

CHAPTER 8

Comparative Analysis with Other Serial Killers

By providing a comparative analysis of H.H. Holmes with other notorious serial killers, we hope to gain further insight into commonality as well as differences among this group of criminals as a whole. Indeed, H.H. Holmes had several features and characteristics that somewhat made him unique among other serial killers, and explorations into corresponding issues will likely figure prominently in further studies about this criminal. For now, depending on one's criteria, it is hard to top either H.H. Holmes as a murderer or for the influence he wields upon the quest to understand the homicidal offender.

has the best non-academically coded biography of H.H. Holmes one can find. Despite being peppered with crimes H.H. Holmes more than likely did not commit, one can at least debate the degree to which the supposedly factual alternates with a too-gory-to-be-true literary genre. Holmes listed at least twenty-seven deaths in his confession, with (soon after) McCrary listing twenty-eight missing persons in a subsequent book. This approach has the curious effect of turning what is commonly called a serial murder, with a high estimate of nine victims, into the deadliest murder spree in American history. Almost immediately after the capture, folks alleged H.H. Holmes was a bigamist, a con artist, and a murderer on the run from out East. It is our hope that further biographies on this complicated figure do not stray far from that fundamental truth as well.

Similarities and Differences

The H.H. Holmes Confessions: Inside the Mind of a Notorious Serial Killer. 8.1. Similarities and Differences. In order to confront the problem of whether the case of H.H. Holmes is best understood as consisting of a variant of a certain type of serial killer or whether he is best conceived as calling for the modification of current ways of profiling such criminals, it is fruitful to consider in some detail the similarities and differences between his crimes and the acts of other serial killers. The goal of this subsection is to provide just such an analysis. In the subsection that follows it, we exploit the understanding of Holmes crystallized in our current account to address the issue of how his case helps inform debates over the definition of the construct of serially violent criminal.

In some of these respects, then, Holmes appears distinct from numerous self-styled "Jack" and "Zodiac" wannabes. Such being the case, one may wonder whether Holmes is instead yet another example of the power-assertive serial killer. Some commentators on violent criminal pathology distinguish between sociopathic power reassurance killers, for whom evidence of their involvement in their own kills (typically brazen, deeply idiosyncratic taunts) is relatively hard to detect, and the arrogant, eponymous power assertive deviants. If we aggregate these two distinct sorts of power killers, then this family of criminal-con artist is the closest available match for Holmes. In fact, the description of his apparent haughtiness can sound almost like a direct quote! In his speeches and personal interactions, Holmes can appear to be "a mild, bold, and gentlemanly sort of fellow," brazenly castigating police for "lack of zeal" in their half-hearted search for his "never to be found" brother during the trial and expressing his trust in God to "bring me through it safely," as well as lamenting the propensity of panicked "jackanapes" to attribute the misbehaviors of "aristocratic English snobs" to "myself and others of English and Celtic blood."

The Holmes Phenomenon in Popular Culture

From a media psychology perspective, there is an interesting phenomenon related to H. H. Holmes that cannot be explained through any extension of general anxiety about hotels and elevators. In the decades following the World's Columbian Exposition, popular culture in America embraced the Holmes story. The deviance of seductive, charismatic monster tapped into a deep, atavistic fear. While this would have been interesting in itself from a sociocultural perspective, the port of Chicago is particularly fascinating because of the variety of literary and filmic A-List treatments that the story has drawn. It is certainly not an exaggeration to describe it as one of the preeminent classical monsters in the American pop psyche. Coming down to the present, Amazon and Apple studios are working on their own Anthology Series and two other books of nonfiction are in the offing.

Simultaneously, Rebecca Dohmen takes the argument for Black Dahlia's resonance and turns it to gender, specifically that Holmes "presents in the public consciousness to balance a movement challenges to traditional power-gender roles: the Cheat, the Con Man, marriages are a fraud," resulting in the need—that is, economic imperative—to silence the voice of the ex-wife. Jill Bumby suggests that it is specifically Holmes' turn toward "modern" murder and his use of newness (pure psychology/genetics, brain surgery, and chemistry) that make him "quintessentially American," to the degree that Holmes and his myth temporarily moved in and skittered across the unsettled landscape of the fin de siècle gotham marketed as "new" itself: Chicago, America's "wonder city."

Books, Films, and TV Shows

H. H. Holmes might be considered the first serial killer as defined by modern experts. The overwhelming evidence results in little doubt that a series of murders were carried out by Holmes. He confessed to them, after all. The question remains: How much of the rest of his autobiographies, written confessions, memoirs, and letters are based on facts? Though many of his post-conviction writings have been proven to be partially or completely untrue, they may have had some nuggets of truth to them. These confessions could also contain much more than details of his killings: the broad strokes of Holmes's childhood and adulthood were likely factual, according to contemporary records.

Holmes's activities became the basis for various horror books, plays, films, TV shows, and even songs and games. It is true, if any serial killer could be said to have a "fan club," it would be Holmes. The very mention of his name becomes a beacon of darkness visited upon an unsuspecting world. He appears overtly in many works, especially in documentaries and shows discussing American murders or architectural horrors. He is often portrayed as being a psychopath, fiendishly clever, charmingly macabre, and devilishly opulent: He resides in his own funfair-like domicile, constructed only for committing ever more torturously intriguing murders. Ultimately, he always falls into his own traps and gets his comeuppance by the end of the film. Typically, he is portrayed by a B actor making use of his talents for leers and charming the ladies.

CHAPTER 10

Forensic Evidence and Modern Techniques

Modern day detectives and forensic scientists have evidence on Dr. H. H. Holmes, including confessions obtained through the use of modern profiling techniques. Forensic evidence on Dr. H. H. Holmes, the man assumed to be Jack the Ripper, does not answer every aspect of his life. What forensic evidence does exist serves to add support to using experiential events to formulate the multiple confessions made to journalists in a pre-Freudian era.

The Victorian influence has presented modern historical investigators with evidence that is not scientific as we would define it. Admissions made by historical figures provide strict "scientific" evidence proving their complicity in the crimes they confessed to perpetrate. Still, little respect has been paid to confessions in the study of historical crime. Applications of modern profiling techniques to historical case studies have brought the confessions of Dr. H. H. Holmes out from the realm of eccentric evangelical confessions into the world of the plausible. Dr. H. H. Holmes' confessions cannot be substantiated with contemporary forensic science techniques, but advances in the field should cause no confusion in his case.

In his time, there likely was no foul play in his prospective "Murder Castle" as forensic science did not exist to effectively track crime. While modern concepts in his case remain limited and highly speculative, some advances in recent forensic science have served to somewhat contribute to the notoriety of Dr. H. H. Holmes. For example, facial approximation analysis has been used to recreate the Doctor's image with his skull acquired, and facial reconstruction on his great-grandson has been attempted. Thus, the mystery of Dr. H. H. Holmes remains transplantation science as the explication of the man's prior life must play on the of-the-alley cerebral box-office.

Advancements in Forensic Science

Before we delve into Holmes' recollection of the crime and modern psychological analysis of his death cell confessions, first we need to understand what modern forensic science has discovered regarding the nature of the "murder castle." Although investigators did not have the tools we have now, it is still one of the first things they thought of and one of the things that always stuck out the most in the case. This was in no small part due to the storeroom of poisons, with bottles bearing the names of his victims. However, at the time of his arrest, a state-of-the-art autopsy was performed on all four members of the Pitezel family.

One of the most valuable tools that we have today is forensic odontology. Many disparaging remarks were written in reference to Holmes at the time that would later indicate a lack of value to himself and family. Based on those documents and witness testimony, the conclusion of the American Dental Association Task Force on H. H. Holmes is that the exhumations in 2017 did in fact confirm the methodology used in the 1895 dental identifications were solid. Dental and medical science knew of almost no ways to tell for certain if a couple of his victims died instantly or not; therefore, many were hard to confirm in later cases. For others, however, time has been a great tool for us to have. We know more about strangulation, poisonings, and blunt instrument trauma today through forensics and postmortem investigations. Back then a clot was the only way to say a victim died of suffocation. Suffocation by gas had no verifiable confirmation back in those days. For poisoning, your asphyxiation had to be self-induced, such as ingesting gas. That was the only way for them to tell for certain that is how a person died back then. Not many of his cases had a distinctive progress of an injury to lead us to a conclusion either. Back then, poisons had to show their effect in forensic tests for poisoning studies. Remember, almost no poisons had a distinctive effect. We have since advanced past that as well.

CHAPTER 11

Conclusion and Final Thoughts

In conclusion, the assertion that the case of H.H. Holmes has been obscured by popular exaggerated mythology is a myth in its own right. The devilish Dr. Holmes was a prolific and thoroughgoing con artist, so why is there so much curiosity about burlesque psychic plots, tarred deer, jumping carcasses, and collapsing houses in his story? Among her countless gyrations, the Black City murderess had accepted the story that Holmes was a much less busy criminal, though this was still almost entirely untrue. As these chapters have shown, one of the remaining and stubborn legacies of the popular version of the Mudgett case has been the distinction between serial murder in 1886, 1892-94, and today, and the transformation of the crime scene in Hyde Park into the so-called "murder hotel."

For those interested in either the history of crime in America or the life of H.H. Holmes, there are still numerous sources that are waiting out there for deep mining. What has often been written off as the mere exaggerations of sensationalism-prone journalists and dime-novelists is, more than likely, anthropological fiction passed down (and possibly even creatively embroidered) as fact by the families of those who played roles in the larger story of the Holmes case.

Throughout his confessions, Holmes embraced the role of the congenital liar and unreliable narrator. This has already been demonstrated in the second chapter of this "confessional," and it is there that there is the most overt evidence of Holmes presenting a deliberately self-defeating tale. As much has been proven, one must need in large measure ignore more or less the whole of the autobiography given for Holmes to have any credibility, and one must begin re-examining the illuminated touches of such a document for what has been concealed or omitted by the teller of the tale, as well as what is demonstrated.

www.ingramcontent.com/pod-product-compliance
Lightning Source LLC
Chambersburg PA
CBHW030414160726
47992CB00007B/3120